MW00761302

# SEASONS OF THE SOUL

Prayers Prose
and
Poetry

BOBBI LEE BYRD

# Seasons of the Soul

Bobbi Lee Byrd

2003

# Seasons of the Soul

Prayers Prose & Poetry

By Bobbi Lee Byrd

Available at CreateSpace.com

Or by phone at (866) 308-6235

$ 12 total cost

sons of the Soul

To: Tia & Jenny

with sincere thanks for
your wonderful hospitality
& thoughtfulness.

Bea & Kim did see the picture
you sent on facebook & all
the comments. Computing was
slow so they plan on sending
a recommendation for
The Highlands Inn in to
the L.C. so you may
want to keep an eye
out for it.

Feel free to add this to
your library if you like

Blessings & hugs,
Bobbi Byrd

R.N.

ᴅᴜᴜ Lk. Rd. S., Osseo, MI 49266 (517) 523-2531

# Contents

## Prose

## Poetry

*This Book Is Dedicated To My Beloved Spouse, Beverly Alleger.*
*You Have Been My Partner In Life For Over Twenty-five Years.*
*You Remain My Inspiration.*

# ACKNOWLEDGEMENTS

Each instrument has a part to play in the Divine Symphony which enriches and compliments the whole. Without each note the music is incomplete. The round sensual depth of Rumi resonates like a saxophone in my middle, then rises up to touch my soul. Daniel Ladinsky's interpretation of Hafiz dances around my consciousness like a playful clarinet and blesses me with an intimate glimpse of the Divine Beloved. The voice of Paramahansa Yogananda is a sweet violin which stirs my heart with the strains of Oneness. The music of their words has roused me from my slumber, and I give thanks for their gifts.

I have been blessed with many wonderful teachers. As a child, I felt inextricably drawn to both St. Francis of Assisi and to St. Theresa. Many years later I discovered that the love and wisdom, which I had found so magnetic, had its roots in their experience of the mystical.

To Sister Mary Kathleen O.P., in whose sixth grade class I read and wrote my first poetry, I say, thank you (even if you were otherwise ornery). Frances Miller, a wonderfully insightful poet, former educator, and friend, kindly offered to help me refine my writing skills. For several years she invited me to her home to "talk poetry." I am deeply indebted to her for her generosity in this regard. Dorothy Hoogterp, Mary Ellen West and the late Ethel Gray-Seese, Terri Jewell and Dora Bradstreet have all been friends and published poets who kept after me to write and to publish my work. Bea Stone and Kim Larabee are both published authors and long-time friends who dared me to stretch and grow by challenging my comfort zones.

Barbara Briner D.O. has been both mentor and friend. Because of her gentle insistence, I began to meditate regularly. As a result, I began to experience a new depth and balance in my life. In the stillness, I finally found my voice. I continue to learn much from you, dear friend. Tony Frudakis, Renee' Mc Millen, Sam Knecht, Chris Sebring, and Steve McElroy, have all been part of an on-going study group of A Course in Miracles . The group has been both a wellspring and a sounding board for my writing. We gather as a circle of friends to learn and encourage one another in our process of re-membering. Thanks and blessings to each of you. I am also eternally grateful to Vivian Frudakis who kindly volunteered many hours out of her own busy schedule to type this manuscript, and to Heidi Greenwood for her computer expertise and assistance with formatting. I say thanks also to my neice, Terra, for her help with computer questions and I'm also sincerely grateful to John Chuchman M.A. for his continued encouragement, suggestions and assistance regarding online publishing. Thank you to Reverend Nan Green, my former pastor, and to all the members of my church family at the Unity Church of Jackson, Michigan, who have welcomed me, taught me, and been supportive of my work. I also wish to extend my sincere gratitude to my entire family who have patiently endured all my early efforts. Their persistent love and encouragement helped make this book possible.

To Beverly Alleger, my beloved partner in life, who for over 25 years has been my best friend, instructor in life, most honest critic, and my model of unconditional love, I say that thank you is not enough. I admire your strength, your compassion and your wisdom. For all the wonderful writers, mystics and friends whose gifts left footprints on my consciousness, I give thanks. Namaste to you all!

# INTRODUCTION

We are surrounded by Wisdom. It can be found in the simplest things, and most often is. It can be forgotten for a while, but never lost. We find ourselves in the position of needing to be reminded of something that we already know on some level. I believe that God has a wonderful sense of humor, and finds myriad unexpected ways to help us rediscover our wholeness and our holiness.

I love the line, "If you want to see God laugh, make plans." Whoever said it, my gratitude goes out to you. We adults take ourselves so seriously. God seems to love to throw a monkey wrench into all our elaborate schemes. Suddenly our vision of reality comes tumbling down like a house of cards. Life is like that. It's about growth, and growth is rarely comfortable. Most of us would prefer to stay in our safe little boxes and predictable routines. Unfortunately, when we spend all of our energy maintaining the status quo, we often miss the unexpected punch line that calls us to new insight. Thus we are not truly engaged in Life's process. One can not coast to the summit. A bit of pedaling is required.

In Neale Donald Walsh's *Conversations with God, Book 3*, the reader is encouraged to stretch limited perceptions and think outside the box. We must each find the courage to reassess our thought systems, and be willing to mature spiritually. (This doesn't mean to become too serious).

God didn't stop communicating with us 2000 years ago. Our understanding of our relationship to our Creator, to one another, and to the world around us has continued to evolve. There is nowhere where God is not. This being the case, how is it that we fail to recognize this Presence? The Omnipresence of God makes all of creation holy and worth reverence. If we are truly made in God's image, then we are actually extensions of Love Itself. How long can we fail to recognize our unity with all this is?

This book is and exploration of my own process. I have known, since early childhood, that Jesus is my teacher. I have taken to heart His promise to be always present and available. I am thankful beyond words for the enduring love of my Creator, and for the guidance of Wisdom. It is my hope that this work will elicit smiles of recognition of our common Life.

Prayers

# Change

Beloved, there is a freshness in the breeze.
I no longer fear the winds of change
but rather, feel exhilarated.
Life has become a wonder filled adventure.
I have decided to let go of my moorings
and to stop trying to buck the wind.
Secure in Your care, I trust the currents.
Let me release the last tethers of fear and mistrust
that I may flow easily in my relationships.
Together we will sail the ocean of Oneness
in perfect safety.

# Come Like the Sun

This morning
I will open the gate of my garden to the Friend.
I look forward to Her coming with joyful anticipation.
I release from my mind all idle daydreams
that I may prepare a place for Her in my thoughts.
I long for the comfort of Her loving embrace.
I treasure these moments of solitude
when we rest in the heart of Oneness.
Come like the sun to my garden.
Burn away the morning mist
and warm my soul.

# Threadbare Past

This day, let me step forward into the present moment.
Let me leave the threadbare garment of my past behind
for it no longer serves me.
As I stand before You in my nakedness
You clothe me in Joy and Light.
You have set Your own seal upon my forehead
so that I may never again lose my way to You.
Father, Mother, God, You enfold me in peace.
You are my home.

# Artisan

Beloved, My mind is filled with so many images.
even as I close my eyes, I can still see them.
I am beginning to understand that what I see
is only a metaphor for what truly is.
As I perceive myself clothed in a physical body
my thoughts weave the tapestry
of the world that surrounds me.
I can choose the colors and the pattern.
Let me not become so overwhelmed by any one thread
that I fail to recognize
Your Omnipresence in all the stitches.
In stillness, show me the beauty of
of what it all means, for I have forgotten Your pattern.
Come, Divine Artisan.
Let me listen to You hum as You work.
Only You can see the finished piece
and know its true value.

# Sufficient

Today I ask for nothing
for I have been given everything.
There is no lack in me
for Your grace is sufficient in every circumstance.
I trust in Your love and abundance.
I allow myself to be lifted and carried
to be immersed in You.
You are my loving Source.
Your Omnipresent wisdom
is everywhere in evidence.
You know my needs.
I trust Your judgment and give thanks.

# Snowflake

This morning, I fall into You
like a tiny snowflake
settling into a vast white carpeted field.
I am content to fulfill my purpose.
All of creation sings Your silent song of AUM.
The universe hums out of earshot of human sense
but it is heard in the stillness of my soul.
Your love encompasses everything
even my dream.
Your peace fills me until I remember
that it is all there is.
Let me carry the warmth of Your love
in my own heart
and extend it without reservation to all.
In the Spring of remembrance the ice melts
and forgiveness blesses the path on which we tread.

# Trust the Seasons

I have enough time
for everything that You would have me do.
Let me focus Your light in the temple of my mind
that with the guidance of Holy Spirit
My thoughts may be one with Your Divine Plan.
May I be the stream bed?
through which Your love flows.
I trust in Your seasons
in the ebb and flow of Your eternal rhythm.
I will dance.
You keep the time.

# Duality

Holy Spirit, let the duality of my experience
give way to the knowledge
that all are One in Christ Consciousness.
Let me cease my judging of good and bad
light and shadow
accepting all that truly is my Self.
Each of us is a unique
and necessary expression of Your Being
wonderful and creative
ever growing
yet always retaining the thread of Identity.
Let me leap with joyful abandon
into the ocean of Your Being.
I trust in You, Dear Friend of my heart.
Let me dive to the depths,
then rise to the surface laughing.
You truly are the color of water
for all can see themselves reflected
when they approach You in stillness.

# Discovery

For a long time I have thirsted
and been unable to quench my thirst
though I have drunk from myriad wells.
I am learning that only the waters of Truth can satisfy.
I have vainly searched
the far reaches of my experience
trying to fill the deep chasm in my heart.
Now I discover that You have waited
silently within its recesses for me to discover You.
In stillness I have found
that the answer to all my desires
lies in my willingness to ask.
Come and make Yourself at home in my heart.
Stay forever...

# Vagabond

Friend of my heart
I will trust all things to Your guidance
for You walk with sure steps
and I would follow Your clear path in the moonlight.
I know that I need not stumble or lose my way
for You whisper clear directions, if I but ask.
I surrender my wanderlust
for I am a tired vagabond.
I long to return to the warmth of Your fire
that we may once again sing the song
that I hear in the depths of my heart.

# Dissolve

Beloved, the winter has been long.
The silence of snow and ice is broken
by the first tiny sounds of Spring's return.
May Your steady warmth dissipate all thoughts
not in accordance with Love.
Dissolve all apparent differences.
Let us flow together like Spring rivulets.
We are the water and You the current and the sea.
Transform the landscape of our thoughts
with Your Spring floods
that we may flow on to our True Source.

# Love is the River

Life is fluid, ever changing in appearance like water.
Only human judgment declares it good or bad
nourishing rain or flood's devastation.
Your eyes behold only perfection
for You are not deceived by momentary circumstance.
Love obeys no rules but its own
and can not be contained.
It flows on
sometimes lingering in quiet pools of reflection
and other times shaping the very rocks
which seem to block its course.
Life is the current and Love, the river.
Let me no longer wait upon the shore.

# Innocence

Holy Spirit, for years I'd closed myself up
fearing that no one could love
the darkness that I'd kept hidden inside.
I had shuttered all my windows and fortified my locks.
Even I could not bear to look upon the monster
that I feared lurked within.

You have been gently calling
trying to waken me from my nightmare.
Gradually, You have earned my trust
as day by day
You coaxed my true Self out of hiding.

The fawn of my innocence has ventured into the sunlight
and I am amazed at its beauty.
Support me as I take my first unsteady steps.
Help me to grow strong in Your Light.

# Home in Your Heart

I am the child who wandered far from home.
All night I have huddled, shivering,
imagining all sorts of fearful creatures
lurking in the darkness.
I am spent from crying.
Silently now, I curl into myself
longing for the comfort of Your arms.
In the stillness I hear Your Voice
and realize that it is You
that I have sought in all my wanderings.
Gather me into Your heart, Beloved.
Only here am I home.

# Persistent Love

Beloved Guest, I am thankful for Your persistence.
You knocked on the door of my heart and waited.
You knew that it had to be opened from within.
At last, I chose to welcome You in.
I had thought myself alone for so long.
As I bask in the warmth of Your Light
and revel in the sounds of Your laughter
all my dark dreams disappear.
I remember only Your company
and the Love that surrounds me
and that I am.
Rekindle Your fire within me
that my heart may be a haven for all.

# Your Vision

Holy Spirit, cleanse my mind and heart
that I may prepare a fitting sanctuary for You within me.
As an extension of the Love and Light
of my Divine Source
I had forgotten my own holiness.
I share this treasured inheritance
for You withhold nothing from Your own.
I depend on Your Vision
to lead me through the darkness
my illusion
to the truth of Love without boundaries
or limitations of any kind.
Heaven lives in my heart if I but open it.

# Tree

This frosty morning
will soon give way to the sun's warmth.
The breath of Spirit stirs the leaves
loosing them to take flight in one last showy bow.
I choose to release my attachment to fame.
I am not the talents, my leaves
nor their fruits, my accomplishments.
I am not the strong limbs or even the sturdy trunk
which has withstood all physical forces of time.
The Tree and I are One
for I dance to the music of the universe.
Deeper than my roots
I embrace my Divine Source
in Whom I live and move and have my being.
I give thanks and praise to You, Beloved.
In You, I am unlimited.

# Wisdom

As I study my face in the mirror
I see that the glow of youth has begun to fade.
The approaching signs of age
are a metaphor for my own inner growth.
I do not begrudge the wrinkles.
With them has come a certain wisdom.
It urges me to look beyond the ego-centered concepts
by which I have lived my life, until now.
The depreciation of my outward appearance
and physical abilities
helps me to realize that I am not the body.
There must be something more.
I have begun to appreciate the quiet moments
for in stillness, I have discovered a Voice within
which calls me to deeper meaning.
The connectedness of all of life
begins to dawn upon my consciousness.
Life has become about sharing the Love that I am.
Lasting beauty can only be found in Oneness.
I was created whole and One with all that is.
I have discovered that the peace
which I had sought for so long
lies within me.
I can experience it only by extending.
This morning I give thanks to my Beloved Source
Who has caused this rose to bloom.
May the aroma bless all with Your Love.

# The Game

Playful Friend,
You have devised a game called physical life.
I am invited to play
and told that I've been given a free shopping spree
in a giant skyscraper of a store.
The only rules are
that I must begin in the basement
shop the entire store, carrying my choices
and meet You on the roof when I'm done.
I begin in a frenzy of excitement
grabbing things from the shelves
trying them on for size.
I have my arms full before I even leave the basement.
I proceed to the next floor
and find items that I like even better.
I begin to discard some of my first choices.
This goes on floor after floor after floor.
There is no time limit to the game
but eventually, my feet begin to get sore
and my arms tire from carrying the heavy load.
Each floor, I leave a few more things behind
until, at last, I have covered the entire store.
I find You waiting with a mischievous grin on the roof.
"Now," You say, " I can keep all I have chosen,
or I can trade it for something
worth immeasurably more behind the curtain."
I choose the curtain.

# Come to Me

Come early to me, Beloved
like the first rays of the sun.
Awaken the sleeping bird of my heart
that it may sing a joyful song
announcing Your arrival.
Let my life ring out the news
of the coming of the Light.

# The Muse

Source of inspiration, Center of my heart
True Light of my mind
You are the Muse.
Speak to me Your words of peace
that comfort and heal all fear-filled souls.
You are the inexhaustible well
which quenches a world thirsty for Love.
It is Your words that I would speak.
Open me that Your Voice be heard.

# Song

Oh Divine Minstrel
You sang me a song
with notes so sweet and so pure
that my heart opened
and I remembered the tune.

# Thirsting for Light

Like the flower that thirsts for sunshine
I look to Your Light, Beloved One.
My petals unfurl in celebration
in thankfulness, opening to Love.
All seeming boundaries gone
flower and light merge
One in truth as they've always been
The daisy, the rose and dandelion
together share the bounty of Your Light.
No single flower
we are Your garden.
Scatter our petals on Loves wedding floor.

# Family Recipe

Beloved, You are the secret ingredient
in the old family recipe.
My soul yearns for the remembered flavor and aroma.
I've tried many concoctions on my own.
They all fall short.

At last, I realize that I can live without it now longer.
I sneak into the kitchen of my heart.
The aroma is much stronger there.
On the counter lays the treasured recipe
and finding it, I smile a secret smile.
A teaspoon of Love was the savory herb that I'd been
missing.
How sweet is my inheritance!

# Ablaze

Beloved Creator
You ignited the spark of my being
from your own eternal fire.
A tiny ember has smoldered within me
awaiting only my willingness.
With conscious intent I invite Your Divine Wind.
Fan Your flame within me until I am totally ablaze in Love
with every shadow of illusion transformed
and every boundary consumed.

# Breathing to Fana

Beloved, dissolve the constructs of my mind
'till words are gibberish and my tongue struck dumb
and I know not light from darkness, amalgam
where no space exists between and we are One.
Even in this state/non-state of being
The Super Nova bursts, extends, extends
in space, and yet I am not absent
for I rest or fly always in Thee.


❧Fana (annihilation in God)❧

# Stillpoint

All of nature has a stillpoint
between the out breath and the in
calmness of the winter morning
before the ice begins to melt.
I stretch this moment a bit longer
revel in the Equinox.
It is here that time is timeless
and Eternity is boundless
the intersecting point and synapse
where I remember all as One.

# What Life is For

As a seed of Christ Consciousness I have within me
the answer to every question posed by life.
You have programmed me to win, eventually
as day by day I recall my gifts.
On my own I try to move a mountain.
Nothing happens but frustration and I learn
that power comes through me and not from me
so I open myself to You (a germination of Your thought).

Remembering is what life is for.

# Immersed

Beloved Creator, immersed in You
Illusions of separateness dissolve to One.
The horizon extends and I recall
the mirror in mirror, infinity
is You, is me, identical.

In Love, conflict can not exist.
No fear constricts this Cosmic respiration.
We flow, become the other with each breath
evaporate, condense, evaporate
One in Thee.

# Ode to Joy

Let me not just talk about joy, but live it
for that is the essence of its gift.
Joy comes from singing the notes
that You have written for me alone.
If I avoid the temptation to improvise
and listen attentively to the subtle nuances of the music
I resonate in harmony with Your Divine symphony.
What joy there is in OM!

# Permanence

Time slips through my fingers like sand.
I close my hand but can not stave the flow.
Shallow roots bind me to Earth
'till Spirit's call reminds me
that only Love remains secure
through time and test of storm.

# Awaiting the Results

The yin and yang of Bush and Gore
Gore and Bush revolve (a giant wheel).
The ancient symbol, light and dark
are two sides of the self same whole
which spin until no clear demarcation
separates the two.

Who can weigh the halves and know for certain
which the greater or the lesser truth to be?
Your Light shines in every heart
though some are heavy shrouded, dark in fear.

Use whichever vessel serves Your hidden purpose, Lord.
May competition be replaced by real cooperation
that each may claim their shadow self
and Love alone claim victory in this election.

# Harbor

Knowledge is a gift beyond perception
offered to all who truly search.
Though perception's persistent practice
leads to the cliff's edge
it is Knowledge which bestows the faith to leap.
Reality speaks not of past or future
nor resembles in the least one's long held views.
It demands a willingness to surrender
a fact which can be unsettling, at best.
The fearful traveler looks to the horizon
and consults all manner of outside clues
yet, only in the chaos of the boat rocked
is the Real Navigator unmasked.

At last the Compass is discovered
within the silent depths of one's own heart.
Yes, the route home is inevitably remembered.
The imagined return has always been assured
for, in Truth, one never left Safe Harbor.
It's impossible to sail beyond Love's reach.

# Celebration

In the sense muffled peace of meditation
I am nurtured.

Gradually, Your Sun rises within me
and the cycle repeats.

Celebration begins at first Light!

# Dampness

Last night's skiff of snow did little to conceal
the brown mountains on the roadsides.
In full sun, dampness forms on the curbs.
Unmanifested rivers of Spring
await but longer days, more Light.
I too pause at the curb
ready to stream out in puddles of Joy.
It will soon be time, for I have discovered
that the ice which I have been
is only You in solid form.
Come Spring
I melt....

# Fragments

No structure of brick and mortar or institution
can lay claim to the entirety of Your Plan.
You speak Truth to all denominations
whispering in the heart of each soul.

We have torn up the map of Heaven
and each holds but a fragment of the whole.
Like squabbling children we cling to tiny pieces
believing that we alone hold the key.

In Light of Spirit let us remember
our way home to one another, and so to You.

# Reminder

Oh Divine Tailor
I am Your creation, wonderfully made.
The fabric of my being is spun of Your very Light.
My design is perfect for every occasion
and my material cannot be stained or torn
or even frayed by constant wear
for it is guaranteed to last forever.
The warranty lies beneath Your label
stitched to the interior of my breast pocket
just over my heart.

I found a note pinned there for my benefit
which reads, "If lost, please return to…"

# Pause

As I exhale, there is a pause
between that which was, and that which is to come.
Yet, there is only this moment, in Truth.
There is a circularity in breathing
(the O of OM).
The in is the out.
One is always contained within the other.
Eternally new, even in its completeness
it continues to expand and grow.

Such is the nature of Love.
Life too is forever fresh and innocent
dawning each moment in the mind of God.
I pause in You and am refreshed.

# Deep Well

My desire primes the pump.
With each breath
I draw Your Living Waters
from the reservoir of my heart.
You rise within me
spilling out in a fountain of Peace.
All creation eddies in the current
joyfully dancing in waves of remembrance.
Come baptize me again in Your Love.

# Newness

Each instant is new, yet ancient.
What is time but a blink in eternity?
Like the volcano which extrudes glowing newness
creation continues its exponential growth, ever outward.
Love expands, collapsing time.
A smile dawns and laughter rings through the ages.
the joy of being has always existed
awaiting only the moment of "re-membrance".
I feel Light hearted today!

# Humbled

Again You have humbled me
But only for my healing.
I trust that You have brought me to my knees
to remind me to ask for help.

Rational thought is a tool
so easily manipulated by my ego.
It "rationalizes" walls
which I have constructed
to protect myself, but from what?
From Love?
From You?

My fears are based on past experiences of pain.
But if I have truly forgiven
why do I still cling to my defenses?

I desire no walls to separate me from You.
Help me to dismantle them
brick by brick
until there is only the Truth
of me in You.

# Aching to Sing

There is a tension in the Earth
a rumbling uneasiness, anxiety.
Its molten depths, emotion's fire
cause breast of mountain's heaving sighs.

Divine magnet tethers Earth to sun
its ancient source of life and light.
Creator kindled primordial orb
and calls it yet to celebrate.

Life's common Source, the Light of Love
extends to Earth, bequeaths a Soul.
Creation together sings one song.
Spirit transcends the physical.
God is! God is...

# Wind

Sea breeze, comb my hair.
Holy Wind, comb my thoughts.
Release, unravel all constraints
until You flow through me
finding no resistance
no hidden fears
clinging tendrils
to keep me from flying free.

Let me soar unlimited in Thee.

# Holey Wholly Holy

I felt holey, shattered, exposed.
You could not enter a closed door.
My heart had to be wholly flung open
for Your Light to penetrate my Soul.

Together we found seeds of Holiness
long buried beneath layers of fear.

Today, You celebrate with me.
Welcome to my healing, Lord!

# Radiance

Beloved,
let me stand naked before You
like the moon
reflecting Your radiance
with no atmosphere of body
to mitigate Your Glory.

Nothing separates me from Your Light!

# Divine Shoe Repair

Like a broken shoelace, held mid-air
in exasperation and surprise
I feel myself detached
and without anchor to my soul.

Walking barefoot in the dark
without my footwear (sturdy soul)
is fraught with painful accidents.
Lord, pity my poor toes!

In meditation, I take time
to retie the knot
which binds me to this Earth Star
and Your Light.

This vital tie needs maintenance.
I must be still, take time and wait
With resolute determination
we reattach my soul.

# I Say / You Say

I say, "There is suffering and terrible agony here
yet, there is also great beauty.
How can both be true?"

You say to me, "Earth is a place of double vision.
You believe what you witness with the body's two eyes.
It seems to be true
because you manifest what you believe in.

The time has come for you to become like a child again.
You must pretend that only Love exists.
It is the only Truth!

The world is innocent of all your bad dreams
and so are you.

There is only One Heart in the universe.
It aches for your return.

Come live again in My Heart!"

Prose

# The Gift

In the Spring of 1964, I was fourteen years old. As the oldest child of a large Catholic family, I had been raised in the Church. I attended daily mass and was in the eighth grade at Our Lady of Victory School in Northville, Michigan. Like many girls educated in parochial school at the time, I had seriously considered entering the convent. The Dominican Sisters were very persuasive. Someday, I hoped to follow in the footsteps of the Saints whom I deeply admired.

None of what I have just related could have begun to prepare me for what I was to witness at the Holy Thursday service that evening in 1964. I had chosen to sit in the front row of the choir loft, located at the back of the church. In the Catholic Church it was customary to have a solemn service on Holy Thursday during which many of the usual adornments in the church are put away or covered in preparation for Good Friday. I remember the altar boys carrying out the heavy candelabras, and the somber atmosphere of the congregation.

As the ceremony progressed, I noticed that there was something very unusual happening. Behind the altar, at that time, there used to be a huge wall of light colored paneling. On it, I began to see scenes, as if watching a movie. There were men and women and children from many different times and cultures. Each was going about their usual daily activities. I remember one man, in particular, tending his store. Judging from his clothing and the items on the shelves, it must have been from over a hundred years ago. Another was a woman, busily cleaning her house. Each person that I saw had one thing in common with the rest. They were each joyfully praising. It was not something that I heard with my ears, but instead, that I sensed with my whole being.

For a moment, I thought that I had fallen asleep and was dreaming. I literally pinched myself to see if I was awake. I was. Then, I looked around the church and wondered why no one else seemed to be paying any attention to all of this. Suddenly, I became aware of a tremendous and overwhelming chorus of praise. It felt like all of creation was joined in this wonderfully joyous celebration of Union. There was no separation between us and the rest of creation. I experienced, in that moment, a deep sense of knowing that this Unity was the Truth of who we are. It occurred to me that those in the congregation, participating in the service, had little understanding of their essential part in what I can only describe as the Communion of Saints. I was deeply shaken by the experience and thought of little else for the next few days.

I decided to discuss my experience with our parish priest, Father John Wittstock during my next confession. He listened as I related this amazing incident, then reassuringly told me not to worry about it. He also cautioned me not to tell anyone else about it. I left the confessional feeling both confused and dismissed. I wondered why this had happened to me, and not to someone older whom Father might have believed. Not knowing what else to do, I did as he had asked, and told no one of my experience for many years.

The spiritual aspect of my being has always been an important focus in my life. I have always had a deep desire to integrate my experiences into an understanding of Truth. In school, the nuns insisted that I take everything they taught, that I didn't understand, on faith, but I questioned perceived inconsistencies. Father Wittstock insisted that Catholic laity not read the Bible, but leave the interpretation of it to the priests and theologians.

I rebelled, and by the age of twenty, I had read the entire text. There were parts that I didn't comprehend, but there was a great deal that I learned from it as well. I remember being awed by this amazing love story of our Creator for a wayward creation. I was deeply moved by the depth and constancy of God's love through so many generations. From this reading, and ever afterwards, I found the message of Jesus, that of inclusive love, to be most compelling. I knew that God's message of love and mercy was meant for all, not just a select few.

My formal religious training clashed with this view, since I'd been taught that only Catholics could go to heaven. I had difficulty with this and a number of other pronouncements made by the Catholic Church hierarchy which didn't jive with my own inner sense of Truth. As a result, despite the fact that I continued to be active in my spiritual and prayer life, I began searching. I attended a Lutheran Church for a number of years, but here too, the concept of inclusive love eventually came under attack. The Lutheran Church had announced a policy excluding active homosexuals from participating in affairs of the Church.

I have come to know a loving God, Who calls me to be the most whole, mature and loving person I can be. I can only do this by being honest about myself. I have no question that God knows and accepts me as I was created, and everything God created was good. I checked Genesis.

After searching unsuccessfully for a church for several years, a friend introduced me to the book *A Course in*

*Miracles*. Though I still didn't have a place to worship, I found in the discussion group of the Course, other people who spoke the same language. Finally, the pieces began to fall into place for me. In the Course, I rediscovered God's Word still active and alive. It spoke of Oneness (the Truth of who we are). To my heart, it was a familiar concept, for I had experienced a glimpse of it. In the confidential setting of our discussion group, I finally related the story of my vision. Soon afterward, I also told my mother, who is still an active member of Our Lady of Victory Church. As the Easter season approached, I seemed to be getting a spiritual nudge from lessons in the Course, that it was time to again reveal my experience to a representative of the Church. I was anxious about doing so, but each day's lesson seemed to be more insistent that the time was at hand.

I decided to attend the Easter Sunday service with my mother. It had been over 30 years since Father Wittstock had admonished me not to talk about my experience. I wondered if he had just not believed me, or if the Holy Spirit had decided that it wasn't time, until now, for the contents of my vision to be revealed. After the service, I met with the young assistant pastor, Father Todd Lajinus. I told him that what I was about to share with him was the truth, and that after much thought and prayer, I had come to the conclusion that it was finally time that the story be retold. I asked him to consult the Holy Spirit for guidance regarding what, if any, action he should take based on what I was about to share. I also assured him that I trusted his judgment in the matter.

In the Spring of 1997, I finally found a Church home, where I feel that I can be a fully participating member of the family. It is also a perfect fit with my own belief system. My spiritual odyssey has, at last, lead me home to Unity. I no longer feel that I must filter out half of what is being preached from the pulpit because it doesn't ring true with my own inner sense of Truth. I know now, that Holy Spirit has been within me all this time, leading me on this, often arduous, journey of my soul.

In April of 1998, I received a wonderful gift of affirmation and confirmation. I was in St. Paul, Minnesota for a conference. While there, I stayed with a friend, Anita Hill, who was then a pastoral assistant at St. Paul Reformation Church. I hadn't seen Anita for nearly twenty years, so we had a lot of catching up to do. The last morning of my stay, I decided to share the story of my vision with her. When I'd finished, Anita gave me a long look and then said, "I want you to follow me to church this morning, before you go to your conference. There is something there that you have to see." When we arrived at the church, she turned on the lights and led me to a spot in front of the altar. As I turned around, I could hardly believe my eyes. There, behind the altar, artists had depicted what I had seen in 1964! The wall was covered with a painting of people from many different times and cultures (men, women and children). Some were even wearing work clothes. The figures were painted on a two story gilt arch which, to me, seemed to symbolically reflect the whole Hosts of Heaven. The front of the altar cloth read, "Praise to the Lord."

I stood there weeping, totally overcome by this beautiful reminder of the gift that I'd been given so long ago. I am at last beginning to understand, that all things happen in God's time. I just need to trust the process.

One question about my experience puzzled me for quite a while. I'd wondered where God had been in this glimpse into Heaven (which is what I believe it was). I think that I have remembered the answer. God was there all along, just not as the separate entity that I had once supposed, but One in total communion with the Mystical Body of Christ (the Son). The Voice for God has brought me home indeed.

# Thoughts on Peace

As our nation is poised, yet again, on the brink of war, I have struggled with my own peace of mind. A Course in Miracles says if we would have Peace, we must teach Peace. We must extend it and become it. It is easy to fall prey to the flash fires of fear that we are bombarded with in the media on a daily basis. Jesus taught us a new way of thinking (forgiveness). It was as radical an idea then as it remains today. "Turn the other cheek," and "Father, forgive them for they know not what they do." He proclaimed Truth in the midst of the apparent ugliness, pain and terror of this world. He saw beyond the outward behaviors to proclaim the inherent innocence of each of us. The Course reminds us that we must learn to see with the same vision. The Holy Spirit shares this vision with the Christ of whom we are each a part.

America is the sole remaining Superpower. As a result, we are in the unique position to change the course of history by proving, once and for all, that might does not make right. I am reminded of a day I watched a big dog sit patiently as he was pounced upon and chewed by a fierce little dog. The big dog knew that he could dispatch the smaller one with one bite, but instead, he just stood up and raised his head, taking his tender ears out of reach of sharp little teeth. The big dog knew that he was not really in danger and he used restraint (forgiveness, if you will). We as a nation can change the world if we learn to open ourselves to the Holy Spirit's guidance. We, individually and as a nation, must exemplify Peace. It is the choice we make in each moment. If we would have it we must extend it. To learn it we must teach it. Jesus never said it would be easy, but we must be the Light of the world.

Poetry

# Meditation

Eyes closed, soul open
immersed in Light of all that is I rise.

I rise and leave behind like cast-off clothes
the weight of mundane day to day
and focus microscope of mind
past cell, atom, to creative Light
the Prime Intelligence
engulfing universe and more.

An awesome exultation
echoes Amen, Amen, Amen...
Beyond imagined time and space
all realms resound in endless praise
for this Light is Love.
This Light is God.

# Beyond Sound

I will listen for what resonates
beyond the world's sounds.
I will not be constrained by mere appearance
for You await me in the silence.
Let me lay my burdened senses by awhile.

When I approach with mind uncluttered
stand with open heart expectantly
I know You'll fill my cup to overflowing.
The bounty of Your love's my only need.

Friend of my Heart, You are the treasure
that nothing on Earth can wrench from me.
I am Yours and You are mine always.
There is truly naught but Thee.

# Live the Dance

I wish to live as a dancer
limbered by life's lessons repeated
until I have learned to bend and not break
supple and strong from a disciplined life
that I may explore new boundaries
without fear of injury.
A grace born of experience
is the genuine love of the dance.

# Perspective

I used to push and stretch and search
for something out of reach.
A stairway adding step on step
ascended out of sight.

Each milestone looked just like the last
(no time to savor goals achieved).
I'd press on, look not left nor right
but simply keep on climbing.

It's only now in retrospect
that I begin to see
why call it fate or what you will
I tumbled from the stair
and landed in a crumpled heap
back where I'd first begun a
and watched dazed in amazement
as the stairway disappeared.

Bruised and battered, though I was
I suddenly could see
a numbered sign that I in haste
had missed the time before
above the open doorway of an empty elevator.
I stepped inside, and with a smile
pressed a button labeled ONE.

# Remember

Seed of Wisdom, predating time
sown in creation's consciousness
grow and blossom
in our attention and desire for Peace.

The ego's trick is slight of hand
a shell game of illusion
which for too long distracted us from Truth.

Let us remember being Love
reclaim forgotten heritage.

What joy there is in Unity.
In Love there is One Mind.

# Hand

A closed fist holds nothing
good or bad
but the hand extended in Love
offers everything there is.

# God's Clothing

We can learn much from our pets.
Look into the eyes of a beagle.
What do you see reflected, but yourself in God's eyes.
Listen to the kitten
sitting in the middle of your "bad news" paper.
Can you hear her purring, "Is that all there is?"
Even the goldfish you watch in its bowl
knows that its sustenance
comes from a beneficent force

(you in God's clothing).

# Safe

I am defenseless
but not vulnerable
for in God am I held safe
from my delusions.

As Spirit
Child of God
forever whole
there is no power
opposed to love.

# In Your Love

Let me see with an inner sight
the beauty of Your glorious Light
shining in each face I meet
remembering they and I are complete
in Your love, in Your love.
We are complete in Your Love.

I have but to change my mind
extend forgiveness and I'll find
the chains of fear I thought bound me
have been released and I am free
in Your love, in Your love.
All can embrace in Your love.

# Timeless Loving

A thousand years are just a day
encompassed in a million years of days
and these last but a moment.

For loving has no time-bound stays
lest it have an ending, terminate
in anything but loving.

# Child of Light

Child of Light be born again
within each mind and heart.
Let the world embrace the peace
that You came to impart.

May Your holy innocence
take root and prosper so
that every face is seen anew
shining in its glow.

Our hearts swell with thanksgiving.
Good news You came to bring
that God created just one Son
and in Him we all sing.

So let us join with Heaven
let all creation praise
for the joy of Christmas
blesses all our days.

# Birthday Song for Jesus

For Baby Jesus angels sing.
Alleluia newborn King.
All the bells on Earth now ring
clanging praise dong ding, dong ding.

Let the music that we bring
echo on the cherub's wing.
Alleluia newborn King
of Earth and sky and everything.

Sing a birthday song for Jesus.
Light his candle, East Star bright.
God's Christmas present to the world
given to us that holy night.

Let the music that we bring
echo on the cherub's wing.
Alleluia newborn King
of Earth and sky and everything.

Alleluia newborn King.

# Little Donkey

Little donkey, did you carry
a young woman great with child?
Could it be her name was Mary
wife of Joseph sweet and mild?

Did you watch with wondering eyes
as you beheld the Infant's birth
or when the angels filled the skies
with Alleluias, Peace on Earth?

Oh, I'll bet you did!

# Rejoice This Easter Morning

You that slumber, awaken!
Open your eyes to this new day.
The gift of your release is offered
free of charge, so celebrate!

Lay down the burdens you carry.
Receive the grace of Easter's news.
Roll back the stone of your resistance.
Accept the Love you seek today.

It has been yours since time began
yet it dawns only in open hearts.
Rejoice, rejoice this Easter morning!
Give thanks for frightening dream's release.

Rejoice, rejoice this Easter morning!
Welcome the One Who is your Peace!

# Senses

My eyes that saw but shadows were mistaken
and ears which heard but insults were deceived.
My nose attuned only to scent of danger
and tongue that tasted but bitterness of tears
had shunned the gentle touch of my Creator
and exchanged His love for frightening dreams.

# Lost Wax

The Jeweler created a beautiful piece
fashioned with exquisite care
a work that reflected a wealth of compassion
a joyful good will and generous spirit
though it was made of wax.

With Divine inspiration the work was soon finished
and casting of plaster was made
then carefully placed in one end as receptor
a crucible filled on the other.

With a searing heat and spiral dance
the wax soon disappeared
but what was left was a ring of gold
when the plaster was chipped away.

The finishing touch, a stone of pure Light
reflecting the Soul of the Artist
was set by the Jeweler
then placed on her finger
to wear for eternity.

# Olfactory Trigger

A plume of aroma
comes rounding the corner
and fills every crevice
from ceiling to floor.

The oven holds essence
of smell's emanations.
The cookies in checker rows
brown 'till just so.

I fill up my nostrils
with whiffs of confections
that tickle my memories
of Grandma and home.

# Packrat

My grandma is a packrat.
I tease her now and then.
She stashes things in closets, drawers
all neat and tucked away
everything from quilting scraps
to folded plastic bags
worn socks to mend
and birthday cards
that crackle now with age.

I was eight years old
the year my grandpa died.
I emptied out my piggybank
and sent Gram all I had.

Yesterday she gave it back
eleven tarnished pennies.
She said, "Do you remember these?"
She'd saved them thirty years.

# Fog

Fog envelops your brain
like the thick white mantle of your hair.
The first strands have multiplied in time
to cover your head and fall over your eyes.

When was it that your mind began to fail?
It's hard to remember
for the mists first crept along the lowlands
and I refused to notice
until they threatened the road I took to reach you.

Looking back, we made light of those first few patches
not wanting to give credence to our fears
but fog continues to roll in.

Each day you wander farther from my voice.
You still recognize the hazy outline of my face
but will you when tomorrow comes?

The reality of this fog disorients me too, and I feel sad
and I'm angry that I can not protect you
and yet, I'm glad that soon you won't realize
that you can no longer live with family.

Today we cling to each other
mingling our tears with the heavy damp.

Damn the fog! Damn the fog...

# Strand of Recognition

Relatives assembled.
Our names and faces, once familiar
shifted in an abstract maze.

Confusion stole my grandmother
her wit reduced to vacant eyes
and her speech to fragments.
We had come like skeptics to a seance
sure her ghost would never speak.

Aunt Loe knelt beside Gram's chair
and captured her attention.
Grandma raised a trembling hand to her white hair
curled a strand around her finger
tucked her thumb into her mouth.
She spoke her daughter's name without a word.
The gesture mimicked Loe as a child.

Her expression changed
began to glow as her eyes found Uncle Bob.
She reached up and stroked his face.
"Tom," she said (my grandpa's name).
That day Grandma remembered some.
It was enough for us.

# For Dad

The rose glow of sunset
has come to rest on the horizon.
I focus on the fading light
and think of you back home.

Before I left, the words flowed
more easily than before.
The memory of those last few days
the love I'll carry in my heart
long after the images of pain fade.

So now, as the sun hovers just out of sight
it colors the sky with flaming embers
deepening blues
beautiful memories of its passing.

Soon I will look to the horizon
and know that you are there
just out of sight
and remember always
the love.

# Patterns

High upon the beach
out of reach of ocean tide's erasure
for at least a generation
maybe two
my father left an imprint
in the sands of time
a casting that will help to mold
the lives of those who follow.

We who remain
trace the pattern with our fingers
and remember.

# My Brother's Keeper

I am my brother's keeper!
I have always been, and yet
I could not keep him from snuffing out his life.

He was my little brother,
sweet, tender hearted
always willing to pitch in and help.

Yes, he grew up on the outside
and pretended he was big and strong like he appeared.

His world became too difficult to bear.
It asked too much!
The pain in others' eyes burned a hole into his Soul.
(The one we all share).

No one thing caused him to lose hope.
He'd lost two jobs, his marriage was faltering
a loved one died tragically
then thousands of faceless loved ones
disappeared in heaps of crumbled ruins.

On a day that would have been Dad's birthday
he forgot the most basic survival tool

(within each heart is the Comforter).
He was so focused on outside pain
that he couldn't find his way Home.

My brother will always be with me.
His smile is etched in my memory
framed in baby curls, childish grins
the love in his eyes when we'd meet.

I will always be his keeper
for he lives now in my heart.

# In Need of Healing

The topic of discussion
was a fragile crystal bowl
dashed upon the kitchen floor
with slivers everywhere.

Our bleeding fingers
torn and pierced
retrieved the scattered shards.
Today, though we are cautious
our bare feet find more.

# Keeping a Straight Face

In a ritual of many years
she'd stand before the morning glass
inspecting curl and painted lips
straightening her seams.

To her students and her colleagues
but most of all to family
she tried to be the epitome
of what they all expected.

As people file into the funeral home
what must they be thinking?
Do they wonder why she killed herself?
Can they look beneath the paint
to see the woman that pain erased
who couldn't live with herself straight faced?

Would they have hired her if she had told them?
Would they have loved her if she had told them?
Would she have killed herself
if only she could have told them?

# Taste of Hats

I like the flavor of a hat
savor the tang and textured spice
it adds to even the blandest stew of days.
The wild mesquite, my cowboy hat
herb of intrigue, my black beret
the cayenne of my red chapeau
cannot compare with the lingering aftertaste
my purple baseball cap creates.
It wrinkles noses for days and days
and surely must be garlic.

# Indiana Pence

There once was a horse of remarkable speed
a black shining beauty, a right handsome steed.
He'd go 'round the track at such a fast pace
he'd seldom ever lose one, no nary a race.

Indiana Pence was the name they would call
and the moment they'd lead him out of his stall
you could tell by the gleam that he had in his eye
he'd let no horse beat him or pass him on by.

He was a track favorite for many a year.
They'd bet on him heavy with nothing to fear.
When you saw one come down
the home stretch by the fence
you could bet your last dollar it was Indiana Pence.

He retired at fourteen, or so I am told
and more years have passed, but he'll never be old
in the memories of all those
who watched this horse race.

Some horses run fast,
but this one could pace!

# Cat and Dog Tale

Every night at half past three
my cat goes on a meowing spree
and races up and down the stair
demanding cat food evening fare.

So insistent in his prowl
inevitably the dog will howl.
At this wee hour he's so demonic
I wish that he was catatonic

and after everybody's up
he goes to sleep after his sup.

# Purrfect Afternoon

I curl in your arms
the cat curls in mine.

Outside, the forest laps a rain shower.
Distant thunder purrs content.

# Living with Plants

I live in a jungle of cactus and fern
with three kinds of ivy that wander and turn.
Begonia, be gone ya' my thoughts were at first
'till blossoms of pink from the frail thing had burst.

Dieffenbachia, Choleus, Wandering Jew
Schefflera and pine tree, Geranium too.

I'm glad you, my friend enjoy every plant.
Lots of fussing and bother, but pretty, I'll grant.
I guess they grow on you.
Plants!

# The Journey

### (A Story of Environmental Illness)

I went to sleep on a quiet sea
but rose to a strange shore
with no memory of the storm
that swallowed up my charts and sextant
and this shipwrecked body, me.

The silent maelstrom tore me from the safety
of my distant moorings.
Home and job, food and clothing, everything was gone.

In days that followed
I explored the boundaries of this foreign place.
I searched in vain the winding streets
for any semblance of home.

The air was thick, lodged in my throat.
The local foods were poison, inhabitants civil enough
if I didn't mention the noxious fumes that they exuded
from vehicles and persons.

I'd blame them for their strangeness, I the interloper.
I'd pout and glare accusing
but it never seemed to phase them.

They decided I was crazy.
It was I who was found different, and it was true.

The maelstrom had happened silently within me.

# 18th Summer

My 18 year old eyes were captured
by the fire of glowing coals, your sunken orbs.
I'd never met someone so old, or so nearly dead.
No flesh at all, how could you live
just skin stretched over fragile bone?

The others said you never ate
but I brought your tray, in case.
I'd rattle on about my world outside your barren walls.
You let me help you with your meals
and because you ate
they let me feed you every day
I worked the summer through.

In time, you sat up in a chair.
We'd talk of baseball and the cat.
He was my very first real pet
but we shared him, you and I.

Then suddenly, you were so ill I was afraid you'd die.
I was scheduled for a trip, but decided not to go.
The morning that I was to leave
you looked lots better, even ate.
You told me, "Go." You'd be just fine.
I wanted to believe you.

(You died the morning that I left
in the middle of your breakfast).

That summer of my 18th year I had made a friend
and found out what it was to lose
somebody that I cared for.

These many years I've thought of you
when I recall the reasons why
I decided to become a nurse.
My list starts with Mrs. Thompson.

# As I Prepare to Say Goodbye

## (Poem for Hospice)

"We've done all we can," the doctor sighed.
    "What happens now?" I thought.
    How can I tell family and friends
    that I'll soon have to say farewell?

"In a hospital bed, with tubes protruding
        from every bodily orifice
    is not how I want my life to end,"
        I heard myself complain.

My nurse suggested Hospice care
    and arranged it with my doctor.
    I can stay home with family
        and live until I die.

A team was formed to address our needs
    care for bodies, spirits, minds.
    I can still have some control
    because I'm a member on it too.

I curl up in my favorite chair
and even hug my dog
while Hospice staff controls my pain.
They're specialists at this.

They support us through our tears and fears.
They're not afraid to talk of dying.
I feel their compassion in hugs and prayers.
Some become like family.

I'm thankful for their TLC
for me and for my loved ones.
It's reassuring that they'll be there
when it's my time to go.

Hospice will help my family
through their first year of grief.
Knowing this eases my pain too
as I prepare to say goodbye.

# Moon Moth

In the velvet black cosmos of summer's night softness
I look to the luminous opal of moon.
I search for the glimmer, the white glowing ember.
I'm drawn like a moth to the lantern of moon.

Careening through darkness, in rapture of kisses
I dance in your pale shining light, Tender Moon.

# Thoughts of You

How often, Love, when you're not here
I feel you close, your presence near.
Frequently throughout my days
to your essence my mind strays.

The tender words and gentle breeze
of your sweet love put me at ease.

So full the joy that I can't measure
or put to words the soul felt pleasure
of your caress and soft embrace
nor in mere phrase describe or trace
even faint outline of how I feel
when thoughts of you upon me steal.

May you know the love I hold
for you alone, and when we're old
in Earthly years we are near done
we'll smile for our love's just begun.

# Your Smile

When first our eyes met long ago
it was as if I'd walked
out of the shade to noon-day sun.
Your smile warmed me so.

# In the Morning

Rise with me in the morning.
We'll leave barefoot tracks in the dew.
Hold me as we watch the sunrise.
Smell summer's faint hint on the breeze.

Let's listen to soft sounds the world makes
as it slowly wakens from sleep.
Rise with me in the morning
and remain in my heart through the day.

# Old Lady Barn

"Poor old lady barn," I heard them say.
How dare they wag their heads at me and sigh!
I have my pride and I won't stand for pity
from the likes of them city folks.

What if my shoulders sag a bit
and knees creak when the wind comes from the North?
I'll admit my joints prefer the warm days
but I've stored such memories in these bones.

In my day, there were no homeless kittens.
They all grew fat and lazy on warm milk.
Creatures large and small would come for shelter
and not a one was ever turned away.

My loved ones are all gone, their children scattered
but their stories linger in my soul.
It won't be long and these new folks will bury
what remains of me and think me gone.

But I will sing them haunting country music
when the night wind whistles through the pine
and fill their dreams with cobweb stands of history.
They'll not forget this old lady barn!

# The Rose

Ask a child to describe the rose of Life
and she will say, "It's pretty and it's red."
She couldn't dream the myriad of shades
that grow beyond the confines of her yard.

Nor is it likely that she's pricked her thumb
on its thorns. At such a tender age
she'd never guess the pain that Life inflicts
on those who come a gardening unaware.

Yet, neither has she stayed near long enough
to become drunk on its perfume
nor to view the world reflected in dew drops
which glisten on each petal in the morn.

She hasn't watched the faded flowers fall
or pressed them between the pages of her book
to recall the splendor of a rose
that was picked so many years ago.

# Embers

Leaves, the dying embers
flame up in Autumn's gusts.
They dance and eddy in the air
like sparks circling.

# By Definition

Fall is
abalone blackbirds
sitting high in golden trees
silver frost on fallen leaves
that grace the floor below
crimson sumac dancing, swaying
to music of the morning breeze
an orchestra of brilliant hues
beneath blue Autumn skies.

# Stay the Warmth

Awaken! Live! Don't sleep too soon.
Summer's warmth is gone. No stay
In fiery heat of red and gold
To keep the wind and snow away.

# Winter Kids

Early we rise to play as two children
to glide in delirium over glistening snow.
We ski 'till our limbs ache
exploring around ice blue lake's
heavy laden evergreens, silent white trails.

With hearts warm as woolen mittens
our faces glow with winter's joy.
We play hide and seek amid the fir trees.
Near forgotten was the game.

Silent magic of the forest
rolls back the calendar of years.
With no grown-up cares to weigh us
We are children once again.

# Afloat

Undulating emerald seas
float farm houses and barns.
The swift current of highways
rush the voyager along.
Cascading torrents fill the sky
and drench us, every one.
Everything on Earth gets wet
when Spring comes sailing in.

# Reflecting Pool

Bare bleached bone
femur of tree
your fleshy bark's a memory
jutting stark from deep green pool
the veil surface dividing.
How fragile is the boundary
the thin film separating
this life from its continuum.
Dare to look.
It bears reflection.

# Distracted

The breeze tickles laugh lines
on the surface of the lake.

Ten turtles form a traffic jam
on a sun-baked log freeway.

A helicopter dragonfly
lights, then flies along the shore.

It's hard to write a serious poem
with all this going on.

# Clouds

Schooners, galleons, clipper ships
all come billowing by
as unseen winds propel them
through clear blue nautical sky.

18704172R00071

Made in the USA
Charleston, SC
17 April 2013